D1407576

EARTH'S CHANGING LANDSCAPE

Expanding Industry

Iris Teichmann

WARREN COUNTY LIBRARY
HEADQUARTERS

First published in 2004 by Franklin Watts
Franklin Watts, 96 Leonard Street, London EC2A 4XD

Franklin Watts Australia
45–51 Huntley Street, Alexandria, NSW 2015
This edition published under license from Franklin Watts. All rights reserved.

Copyright © 2004 Franklin Watts

Series Editor: Sarah Peutrill; Series Designer: Simon Borrough; Art Director:
Jonathan Hair; Picture Researcher: Juliet Duff; Series Consultant: Steve Watts,
FRGS, Principal Lecturer in Geography Education at the University of
Sunderland

Published in the United States by Smart Apple Media
1980 Lookout Drive, North Mankato, Minnesota 56003

U.S. publication copyright © 2005 Smart Apple Media
International copyright reserved in all countries. No part of this book may be
reproduced in any form without written permission from the publisher.

Library of Congress Cataloging-in-Publication Data

Teichmann, Iris.
Expanding industry / by Iris Teichmann.
p. cm. — (Earth's changing landscape)
Includes index.
ISBN 1-58340-481-3
1. Industries—Environmental aspects—Juvenile literature. I. Title. II. Series.

HD30.255.T445 2004
363.73'1—dc22   2004040193

9 8 7 6 5 4 3 2 1

Picture credits:
Toby Adamson/Still Pictures: 12b, 31b. Mick Blowfield/Ecoscene: 27t. Joerg
Boethling/Still Pictures: 34c. James Davis Worldwide: 18t, 33. Digital Vision: front
cover, 1, 2, 8t, 9r, 16, 17, 22tl, 23r, 24b, 26l, 27b, 29l, 29t, 38r, 39b, 40t, 41t, 47, 48.
Stuart Donachie/Ecoscene: 39t. Mark Edwards/Still Pictures: 26r, 30t, 42c. Mary
Evans Picture Library: 6. Chinch Gryniewicz/Ecoscene: 14-15. Michel Gunther/Still
Pictures: 32c. Ian Harwood/Ecoscene: 32b. Peter Hulme/Ecoscene: 25. Laura
Jones/Eye Ubiquitous: 21b. Martin Jones/Ecoscene: 20b. Ed Kashi/Corbis: 35b.
Klein/Hubert/Still Pictures: 24c. Matt Meadows/Still Pictures: 10t. Tim Page/Eye
Ubiquitous: 36c. Edward Parker/Hutchison Library: 37b. Harmut Schwarz-
bach/Still Pictures: 43c. Vince Streano/Corbis: 11b. Topham/AP: 19b. Topham
Picturepoint: 13b. Visual & Written/Ecoscene: 22r. Jim Winkley/Ecoscene: 7b.

CONTENTS

THE INDUSTRIAL REVOLUTION

For thousands of years, people have engaged in industry—the manufacturing of goods and services. Our planet is full of useful resources, and people have learned to use these in different ways. Industries have expanded, changed, and diversified, transforming the land beneath and around them in the process.

Primary industry The oldest kind of industry is obtaining and using raw materials—also known as **primary industry**. For thousands of years, people have cleared land for farming, cut trees to get wood, and extracted minerals from the earth.

Secondary industry In **secondary industries**, people process raw materials into products that are of use to them. The time period when this began on a large scale is called the Industrial Revolution. Britain was the first country to industrialize, beginning in the 1780s, followed by mainland Europe and the North American continent during the 1840s and 1850s. Manufacturing developed quickly as people invented big, efficient, power-driven machinery.

Industrial scene in the Ruhr region of central Germany. The area was the most important industrial region in Germany during the Industrial Revolution because of its coal reserves.

Follow it through: industry location

Water powers machines for industry

Industrial villages are settled near rivers and canals

Heavy and light Secondary industry can be put into two categories: heavy and light. **Light industry** processes light raw materials. The textile industry—processing cotton and wool into fabrics—was an important early light industry during industrialization. The most important **heavy industry** was the iron and steel industry—the extraction of coal and iron ore to make steel. These industries changed the landscape in a way that still affects us today.

Industrial villages In the early stages of industrialization, waterpower was one of the main sources of energy. Factories were built along rivers and streams where huge waterwheels would drive the machines.

In turn, factory owners built houses for their workers next to the factories, creating the first industrial villages. These villages were a key feature of the landscape in industrializing countries.

Steaming ahead The invention of the steam engine started a second phase of the Industrial Revolution. However, a lot of fuel was needed to power steam engines.

Experts think that one reason Britain was one of the first countries to industrialize was that many of the forests had already been cleared, and coal was an important fuel source. Britain had large coal deposits and was able to use these in its iron and steel-making processes. As a result, new factories were mainly located next to coalfields.

Case study: Saltaire, West Yorkshire, UK

The village of Saltaire was built between 1851 and 1876 around its large textile mill.

World heritage site
The mill owner, Titus Salt, built the village around his mill to house his workers and also built churches, schools, and parks. The houses are still in use today. The mill was in disuse until recently, when it became a world heritage site. It now contains shops, businesses, and art galleries.

The mill stands out clearly on Saltaire's skyline.

Industry advances

Steam power-driven machines are invented

Exploitation of coal increases

Iron, steel, and other industries relocate near coalfields

Bom Futura Tin Mine, Brazil. Brazil is a leading country in the extracting of minerals such as tin, iron, and gold. This involves clearing large areas of rainforest.

MINING

Making use of Earth's natural resources has been an important activity for thousands of years. People have dug up stones and clay to build homes. They have searched for metallic minerals such as iron and bronze to make tools and jewelery. But it has been since industrialization that our search for Earth's resources has had the greatest impact.

Changing the landscape

The iron, aluminium, and copper mining industries have been, and continue to be, important primary industries because these minerals provide the raw materials for many products.

Extracting large amounts of mineral deposits inevitably affects large areas of land. To prepare the land for mining, forests, farmland, or vegetation have to be cleared. It may even involve changing the courses of streams or rivers. If the area is inhabited, homes have to be moved elsewhere, and roads have to be diverted.

Follow it through: effect of mining

Minerals are found and a site is developed for mining

Soil conditions change
Rivers are moved
Landscape changes

Surface mining

Many minerals—such as copper, limestone, and some types of coal—can usually be found just below Earth's surface. To get to these minerals, large amounts of topsoil have to be removed. If the deposits are in a hillside, it means removing the hilltop. Sometimes, explosives have to be used to break up the mineral deposits.

This type of mining is called opencast or **surface mining**. Surface mining can transform large areas of land. For example, the Bingham Canyon copper mine in Utah covers an area of 3.2 square miles (8.5 sq km).

Underground mining

Some minerals, such as certain types of coal, sit much deeper below Earth's surface. In order to get to them, vertical shafts equipped with an elevator are built from the surface down to the level where the coal is situated. This type of mining is called **underground mining**. Water has to be pumped out to get to the coal, causing groundwater levels in the area to fall. Nearby plants and trees may not be able to reach the lower groundwater levels and may die. The upper layers of the soil may also erode, causing **land degradation**.

Slag heaps

To extract minerals, large amounts of soil and sediments are removed. Mineral deposits have to be cleaned, which causes rock waste to accumulate. These are usually piled to form **slag heaps**.

Once all of the mineral has been extracted, slag heaps may be used to fill the pit. However, some may also be carried into rivers, which then fill with the sediment. This can change the river's course and lead to a change in vegetation along the riverbank.

Land recovery

Land that has been mined can be transformed after the mineral has been extracted. In the traditional Ruhr mining area in central Germany, disused mining areas have been turned into recreational parks with lakes and trees. It takes at least 15 years for land to recover, however, as new plants and trees have to adapt to the new soil.

An opencast limestone **quarry** in the Yorkshire Dales, UK. Quarrying provides jobs and income for the region, but it makes a large area of landscape become a barren eyesore.

Vegetation and wildlife are disturbed

Minerals eventually run out

Slag heaps remain

Land needs time to recover

INDUSTRIAL CHANGE

The iron and steel industry powered the Industrial Revolution of the 19th century in Europe and North America and continued to be important well into the 20th century. But during the 1970s and 1980s, the industry declined rapidly in many places, leaving behind abandoned industrial sites.

Acidic **run-off** from an abandoned mine in the U.S. has polluted this wetland area.

Running out Many towns across Europe and North America were built around areas with large coal deposits where iron and steel companies operated. After decades of exploiting the coal and iron ore, companies found that these resources began to run out. Importing coal from other areas was often too expensive because the factories were situated far away from other cities and ports.

Competition At the same time, countries in parts of the world such as Australia, China, India, South Africa, and Russia began to exploit their own coal and iron ore resources. They are currently, together with the U.S.—which still has large coal reserves yet to be exploited—the major coal exporters worldwide.

Japan was one of the first countries to combine the different production processes for making steel into one large site and locate them at ports for easy transport. For that reason, Japan was able to produce steel much more cheaply and efficiently than countries such as Britain and the U.S. As these and other countries gradually moved steel production to ports, more steel became available on the global market. This, in turn, lowered the price for steel, and steel production became very competitive.

Follow it through: industrial change > Natural resources are depleted > Transporation costs to get raw materials to the factory increase >

Closing down Steel factories in Europe and North America began to close down. The sites often became neglected, and rail links that served the steel industry were mostly closed down. Other types of industries were not willing to locate in these run-down areas.

As a result, many such areas continue to be derelict. These sites can cause environmental hazards such as metal waste or leftover chemicals affecting soil, vegetation, natural waters, and wildlife. Derelict industrial sites can also cause the surrounding areas to become run-down as people leave in order to find work elsewhere.

New competitors

As manufacturing industries began to decline in industrialized countries, they began to increase in less economically developed countries, such as Thailand and China. There, industries could take advantage of a cheaper workforce to produce goods more cost-effectively.

An abandoned steelmill in New Jersey. Many old steel plants in New Jersey have now been regenerated *(see right)*.

Case study: New Jersey

New Jersey has many disused industrial sites where manufacturing and steel factories have closed down, but efforts are being made to redevelop these areas.

New developments
In Trenton, for example, an old steel plant site has successfully been turned into a baseball field. New housing and office buildings have also been built. The new developments themselves attract even more redevelopment. There are plans for a new shopping center and new businesses. As a result, the whole area is gradually changing into a modern business area that offers housing, leisure, and shopping facilities, and attracts not only more business, but also workers to the area.

Production becomes expensive ➤ Prices increase ➤ There is less demand for the product ➤ The factory closes or relocates

CHANGING LOCATION

With the invention of mass production techniques in the early 20th century, factories became bigger, and many moved to new locations. With better transportation, factories could now sell their goods in other parts of the country and in foreign countries as well.

Pudong special economic zone, Shanghai, China. Such zones have been set up in many less economically developed countries to encourage investment from foreign countries.

More space Some factories needed to move to less built-up areas where there was more space. In New York, many of the small factories and warehouses that operated during the early industrial era moved to smaller towns in the south of the country. There, they had space to expand, and people worked for much less money.

Going global Today, more economically developed countries (**MEDCs**) have moved some of their production plants even further away—to developing countries where production is even cheaper.

For example, a global map of the textile industry would show that most clothes are made in less economically developed countries (**LEDCs**) such as Mexico, China, Bangladesh, and Thailand. These countries have a large pool of cheap labor available and a good infrastructure in and around their major cities.

Follow it through: industry in LEDCs

LEDCs have a cheaper workforce

They can produce goods more cheaply

At a price Industrial development involves using more land for building factories, transportation networks, and other facilities. In developing countries, industries have mainly been expanding on the outskirts of major cities, putting pressure on the surrounding land.

About 30 percent of Thailand's economic output is produced in industries around Bangkok. The city has expanded so much that the Thai government is trying to reverse this trend by encouraging industries to locate in rural areas in the south of the country.

In China, large amounts of forest were cleared for industrial and urban development along the Yangtze River that runs through central China. This left the riverbanks exposed and soil—no longer held by tree roots—was washed into the river, causing major floods. The Chinese government has now started a reforestation program, intended to replant some of those forests to avoid further floods.

Take it further
Find out what the most important industries are in your area.

◆ What types of industries are they?
◆ What do you think are the main reasons for being located there?

The area around Bangkok, Thailand, experiences congestion due to the high number of industries in the region.

Case study: special economic zones, Honduras
Less economically developed countries actively encourage foreign firms to invest in their country by designating certain areas as "special economic zones"—areas where foreign firms can build their production plants without having to pay taxes.

Major developments
In 1977, Honduras created its first special economic zone in the port town of Puerto Cortes. Today, there are nine such zones along its northern coastline. It is a major area of development for more than just industry. Infrastructure has been improved, and more housing has been built for the increasing number of workers it attracts.

Industry moves to LEDCs

More land in LEDCs is used for industrial development

Infrastructure and transportation in LEDCs improve

Industrial regions decline in MEDCs

13

GLOBALIZATION AND THE FOOD INDUSTRY

In today's global economy, countries buy (**import**) and sell (**export**) goods and services both to and from other countries. They can make money by exporting goods, and they can then spend that income on expanding their industries. In the last few years, LEDCs in Africa and Asia have adapted their land use in response to global market forces.

From small to big

The food industry in more economically developed countries is dominated by a small number of big retail industries. These give contracts to the cheapest local food distributors in less economically developed countries.

Because of the price competition, only large farms that produce high enough quantities of their produce make enough money from selling to the local distributors. Specialization in the food industry in these countries has led to intensive farming, called **mono-cultures**.

Follow it through: intensive farming

Farming is a key part of an LEDC's economy

To earn extra money, LEDCs farm "cash" crops for the export market

Monocultures In a monoculture, only one crop is grown, usually over a large area of arable land. Intensively growing one crop takes nutrients from the soil, and it becomes less fertile. Growing on a large area of land usually involves clearing the land of trees, hedgerows, and other vegetation. This exposes the soil, dries it out, and causes it to erode. Farming intensively also involves the use of fertilizers and pesticides that can contaminate the soil and harm wildlife in the area.

Kenya now specializes in growing and packing green beans and flowers for export to big retailing industries in Europe. The land around the Naivasha freshwater lake, northeast of the capital, Nairobi, was once used to graze animals. Today, the area is intensively farmed, and green beans are grown in large greenhouses. The lake's water levels are falling, and the water is polluted from pesticide use.

Lake Naivasha, Kenya, where flowers and green vegetables are produced for export to European markets. It is the major source of employment in the area, particularly for local women.

Intensive farming of single crops, called monocultures, occurs

Soil is exposed and its nutrients are exhausted

Soil erodes

Fertilizers are needed

URBANIZATION

During the Industrial Revolution, people moved to urban areas to work in the factories. Cities and towns became bigger. Today, this trend of urbanization continues—particularly in less economically developed countries—as millions of people **migrate** from the countryside to the cities in search of work in industry.

An industrial plant in California. Farmland in the U.S. is being squeezed because of urban sprawl, and much of the country's food production is done on farms in close proximity to urban areas.

Urban sprawl Experts estimate that half of today's world population lives in urban areas.

Even in developed countries, where the population growth has remained stable, more and more land around cities is being developed. As Chicago expanded from 1970 to 1990, statistics show that 74 percent more land was used for industrial and commercial use, yet the city's population grew only slightly.

Urban sprawl—the growth of cities into the surrounding green space—causes valuable fertile farmland to be lost. This is because many cities were originally settled in low areas near rivers, where the soil was very fertile.

**Follow it through:
urbanization in LEDCs**

Industries expand on the edge of cities

People migrate from rural areas to urban for work

Shrinking wetlands Europe is a very densely populated continent compared to North America or Australia, and around two-thirds of **wetland** areas have been cleared for industrial and urban use over the last two centuries.

In parts of Europe, this has led to an increase in floods. Industrial sites, housing, and roads have replaced large areas of river floodplains. Heavy rainfall can no longer sink into the ground on these surfaces, and instead it runs off into rivers, causing floods and mudslides.

The European Union has taken steps to promote more development of green space in urban areas. In Eastern Europe, however, forests and other natural areas continue to be cleared for their expanding industries.

City slums Cities grow at a faster rate in less economically developed countries. Often, this is caused by the migration of poor farm workers from the countryside, as they move to work in city industries.

The official population in Addis Ababa, Ethiopia's capital, is 3.5 million, but there are also an estimated 1.5 million people who live in slums on the edge of the city. They have no access to clean, running water or other facilities in the way that other city dwellers do.

A shanty town in Manila, Philippines. Many cities in less developed countries cannot cope with huge numbers of people from the countryside arriving to find work. Migrants end up building shelters on unused land close to the city.

Urban area expands

Shanty towns are built

Farmland is lost

Better city infrastructure is needed

THE SERVICE INDUSTRY

The majority of the developed world's industrial output today focuses on the **service industry**, called tertiary industry. Tertiary industries include the financial sector, such as insurance companies, banks, law firms, and accounting firms, as well as the tourist and leisure industry.

Manhattan, New York. This area provides office and working space for the world's biggest global companies working in the financial and business sectors.

Business first City centers in cities such as London or New York can no longer support the presence of traditional secondary industries like they once did during the Industrial Revolution. There is not enough space for modern, large-scale industrial plants. Land in cities has become too expensive, and pollution from industries would not be acceptable to the people living in the cities. Today, it is service industries—especially banks, management firms, and law firms—that have located in inner-city areas. Because space is limited, office buildings are often built upward.

Follow it through: service industry

Heavy industry moves to LEDCs

Service industry grows in MEDCs

City centers change and redevelop

Attracting more investment
Commercial city centers usually have good transportation and also attract other smaller businesses into the area, such as bars, restaurants, shops, and leisure facilities that city workers use during the working week.

On the edge
With the emphasis on service and **retail industries** in city centers, other industries had to expand on the outskirts of cities, especially on the fringes of suburban areas. When industries encroach on rural land bordering suburban areas, the development of housing, roads, and shopping centers often follows.

The Washington–Baltimore corridor in the U.S. has seen major development of industrial sites, road networks, and other facilities, including two airports.

Case study: Barcelona, Spain

Barcelona embarked on a major redevelopment within its perimeters when it prepared for the 1992 Olympic Games.

Industrial decline
The site of the Olympic Games became available a few years earlier when old textile factories and gas companies closed down. The authorities declared the area as a tourist and residential zone. New housing complexes were built, hotel and other service facilities created, and the derelict waterfront was turned into artificial beaches and paved relaxation areas.

After the Games
The city had reached development limits, and transportation was not sufficient to ensure good access into the city and the redeveloped area. Barcelona is now working on redeveloping a large area to the north of the city by encouraging tertiary industries such as hotels, shops, leisure facilities, and offices. It is even reclaiming land from the sea in the process.

Barcelona's Olympic stadium was built on a large, disused industrial site.

Some industries are established on the fringes of suburban and rural areas

Shops and leisure facilities increase in city centers

Transportation to and from city centers needs to be improved

BROWNFIELD SITES

Many countries today have large numbers of industrial sites that once were active but are now abandoned. They may be small sites such as disused gas stations or shops, or big sites such as large factories or warehouses. These sites are called brownfield sites.

An oil depot site that has been abandoned.

Contaminated?

One of the major problems with brownfield sites, especially those that were once the site of a manufacturing or chemical plant, is that the land may be contaminated. For example, the soil and groundwater in and around the land may contain leftover metallic substances, oil, petroleum, or other organic material. Brownfield sites often have a lot of garbage, old pieces of metal, storage facilities, and other waste material lying around.

Reusable?

Very often, brownfield sites were sites of major industrial activity during the height of the Industrial Revolution. This means that they are likely to be located in or near town centers and can be valuable. However, clearing contamination so that the site can be reused for something else can be very expensive.

Follow it through: brownfield sites

Industrial activity declines

Cities are left with abandoned brownfield sites

Good neighborhood? If a brownfield site has been neglected for a while, it will affect the surrounding area as well; it may decline and become unattractive for private housing. However, in some cities, such as New York, large warehouses have successfully been turned into modern apartments to accommodate people working in the city.

Take it further
Locate a brownfield site near you. Find out what is happening to it.

◆ Is it still being neglected or is it earmarked for commercial use or new housing?
◆ What do you think would be the best solution for it?

Case study: two power plants, London, UK

Battersea power plant
On a large brownfield site in south London stands the now-disused Battersea power plant. It is a listed building, which means it must be protected because it is of historical value. One developer tried to turn the site into a movie theme park but ran out of money. The site is large, and years of neglect have meant that the area around it has not been regenerated. Currently, a group of developers is working on ideas to modernize the site.

Tate Modern, London. The redevelopment of the Tate building has led to the redevelopment of large portions of the riverbank area.

Tate Modern
In contrast, the Tate Modern, by the river Thames, was a coal-fired power plant that now houses a large collection of international modern art. The building was unused for 13 years after the plant closed in 1981. However, its central location and large floor space meant it was an ideal location for a gallery. A total of $236 million was spent on the construction, which took five years. Today, the Tate Modern is a key attraction for British and foreign tourists.

Brownfield site is contaminated or too expensive to modernize ▶ Site is left abandoned

Site is modernized ▶ Site enhances the area

THE ENERGY INDUSTRY

Since industrialization began, the demand for energy—both by consumers and industries—has increased substantially. Because the world's existing coal reserves are being depleted, and also because burning coal may cause climate change, other types of energy industries have started to become important.

An oil platform in the North Sea. Most oil is found under the sea bed, where it formed millions of years ago.

Oil and natural gas Much of our energy today comes from oil and natural gas reserves. Some drilling occurs offshore, but drilling for oil on land has more impact on the landscape. Oil fields are created by drilling more than 160 feet (50 m) into Earth. Pipelines are laid to transport the oil across large distances.

Oil disasters Each year, an average of 17 million gallons (65 million l) of oil from more than 10,000 accidental spills get into freshwater and saltwater environments. This not only harms natural ecosystems, but also affects human environments such as coastal resorts. In 2002, the oil tanker *Prestige* sank off the northwestern coast of Spain, spilling more than 70,000 tons of oil into the sea and damaging beaches and wildlife in the area.

Workers clean up oil on the coast of Spain after the *Prestige* disaster. A large oil spill at sea can devastate coastal areas, fish, and wildlife. But much smaller oil spills also happen on a daily basis when oil is accidentally spilled as it is extracted.

Follow it through: energy

Industrial activity increases globally

More consumers use more energy

Demand for energy increases

Nuclear power

Experts think that to meet future demand for energy, the world needs around 12,000 nuclear power plants. Nuclear power is clean and efficient and does not produce greenhouse gases. It is created from uranium, a radioactive metallic element. Radioactive materials can cause damage to plants, wildlife, and humans if they are exposed. Depending on weather and wind conditions, the ground up to about two miles (3 km) around a nuclear power plant can show high levels of radioactivity.

Nuclear power is also problematic because it creates highly radioactive plutonium waste that is difficult to dispose of. It can take several hundred years to degrade and become harmless.

Hydroelectricity

The flow of water in rivers and streams can also be turned into a form of energy called **hydroelectricity**. The power of water is a renewable energy source, since the water itself is not being used up. Hydroelectric power plants are very useful to industries because they can create huge amounts of energy. A big hydroelectric plant can provide electricity for an entire city. The U.S., one of the biggest consumers of energy worldwide, already gets 10 percent of its electricity from hydroelectric power plants.

Building hydroelectric plants has a huge impact on the landscape. Plants require dams that allow water to collect in reservoirs. Building dams, however, changes the course of a river and affects the surrounding land and wildlife. The building of the Tucurui Dam in the Amazon, Brazil, destroyed large areas of rainforest and also caused an estimated 78,000 people to lose their homes.

Dumped equipment next to the Chernobyl nuclear power plant, Russia, where there was an accident in 1986. Experts think that the area will remain radioactive well beyond the 21st century.

Take it further

Do you know which electricity sources provide the energy in your home?

◆ What electricity sources are there in your area?
◆ How do they impact the land?

Non-renewable energy resources are limited

Carbon emissions increase

Nuclear and hydroelectricity energy use increase

May also cause large-scale environmental damage

ENERGY ALTERNATIVES

Around 80 percent or more of the energy used around the world comes from three **fossil fuels**: coal, oil, and natural gas. Although they are natural energy resources, they are non-renewable, because they will one day run out. They may also cause global warming (*see pages 28–29*). Since hydroelectricity, although renewable, causes massive changes to the landscape, industries are investigating other renewable energies.

Solar power plant, Australia. Countries in warm climates have great potential for exploiting sun energy.

Solar energy The warmth of the sun can be converted directly into electricity by using solar panels. These are used increasingly when new homes are built but, at the moment, are not powerful enough for industrial use and do not work well on a cloudy day.

While large solar power plants can have a visible impact on the landscape, they tend to be built in low population areas. They can also be built into existing marks in the landscape. In Switzerland, solar panels have been placed at regular intervals along highways.

Wind turbines providing energy in the San Gorgonio Pass, California.

Wind power Many countries, such as Denmark and the Netherlands, have built wind turbines to turn the wind into electricity. Wind farms can be very effective, but they can also be controversial since they are often built in areas of natural beauty, such as mountain areas and coastlines.

Wind turbines need to be built into large holes. This can damage groundwater flows and destroy wildlife.

Follow it through: energy changes

Fossil fuel energy sources are finite

Nuclear and hydroelectric plants are controversial

Geothermal energy Deep inside Earth, water is heated by hot, melting rock. By drilling down to this water, **geothermal** energy can be obtained. Geothermal energy also comes in the form of heated steam extracted from rocks. Both are piped to drive turbines that produce electricity.

The biggest geothermal power plant of this kind is in California. It produces as much electricity as two nuclear power plants. Iceland is a leading country in using geothermal power to heat homes.

The extraction of geothermal energy, however, can produce small amounts of carbon emissions that are thought to be the key cause of global warming. Some geothermal wells can also cause the land above to subside.

A geothermal power plant in Iceland. It pumps cold water into the ground, which then heats up. This water is then pumped out to be used over long distances. At the same time, the plant gives locals and tourists the chance for a hot bath!

People explore renewable energy sources

Their effectiveness and overall impact on the environment has yet to be fully explored

INDUSTRIAL EMISSIONS

Experts estimate that industrial production worldwide emits more than a hundred different substances into the atmosphere. What industries emit depends on individual production methods and the environmental standards that are set by governments.

Acid rain By looking at the smoke coming out of the chimney of a large chemical industrial plant, one can see that its emissions can spread easily across a large area, particularly if there is any wind.

In the early 1970s, scientists in central Europe discovered that chemical emissions were causing large areas of forests to become damaged by "acid rain." When fossil fuels are burned to produce power, a gas called sulphur-dioxide escapes into the air. This falls onto tiny cell gaps on leaves and pine needles and turns into acid, destroying the cell structure of the leaf. The gas can also dissolve in rain, making it acidic. The acid rain then falls onto the soil, reaching into the roots of trees and other plants. The chemical, paper, metal, coal, and petroleum industries are the main contributors to acid rain, but government restrictions are now in place to attempt to regulate emissions.

Pollution from industry such as this cement factory (*left*) has caused damage to trees by acid rain (*right*).

Follow it through: acid rain

Factories emit acidic chemicals such as sulphur dioxide

Some acids end up in the soil

Some are spread by the wind and mixed with moisture in the air

Polluted waters

Most industries use water during the production process, and this can get contaminated with industrial substances and then discharged into the environment. Different substances have different levels of impact. Metallic substances, such as mercury, are particularly toxic. In natural waters, metallic pollution is impossible to clean up. Over time, if pollution levels increase, fish and wildlife will die.

Less economically developed countries suffer severely from industrial pollution. In Delhi, India, industrial waste is regularly emitted into the Yamuna River because it is cheaper than cleaning the water, even though there are laws in place to stop such practices.

A boat crossing a river polluted with soap suds in Jakarta, Indonesia.

Case study: the Ozone Layer

Scientists discovered in the 1970s that industrial emissions were contributing to a thinning of the ozone layer over the Antarctic. Ozone is a layer of gas around Earth's atmosphere that protects the planet from the sun's harmful solar radiation.

Reducing emissions

Since the discovery of the ozone's hole, many countries have regulated their industries, and there has been a considerable reduction in the gases that are thought to have caused the thinning of the ozone layer.

Ozone may also be thinner over the Arctic. On this map, the most concentrated levels are in red and yellow.

Industrial waste

Many industries burn their industrial waste. This causes gas emissions that escape into the atmosphere and then fall to the ground, contaminating the soil.

Other industries use landfills where waste is buried. Although this takes up land, it can eventually be recovered and re-landscaped for other uses.

Rain mixes the chemicals with soil

Acid rain falls

Soil becomes acidic, damaging tree roots and limiting plant growth

Acidic deposits damage leaves, trees, and plants, and further acid mixes with the soil

CLIMATE CHANGE

Earth has always been subject to climate change. The last most significant change was during the Ice Age around 15,000 years ago. Over the last few decades, there has been a slight, but significant, increase in global temperatures that many scientists believe is due to industrial activity.

What are the causes? Scientists today mainly agree on the most important factor contributing toward global warming: the burning of organic materials such as coal, natural gas, and oil. These contain carbon that is released into the atmosphere as **carbon dioxide** when these fossil fuels are burned to produce power. Carbon dioxide is called a greenhouse gas because it helps to trap the sun's heat inside Earth's atmosphere.

It is thought that the levels of carbon dioxide in the atmosphere have doubled between the start of the Industrial Revolution and the 21st century. These increased levels may cause Earth to get warmer by around two degrees, if not more.

The consequences? Scientists do not agree how much global warming has affected Earth, or will affect it in the future. Some believe that an increase in extreme weather, such as floods and hurricanes, is a direct result. Some predict that a warmer Earth surface will cause more severe droughts in tropical and dry climatic regions where there may be less land available to grow food. In colder climates, more land may become useful for farming.

As it gets warmer, glaciers and ice caps will melt, causing global sea levels to rise. This will threaten low-lying land such as islands, coastal areas, and countries already susceptible to frequent flooding, such as Bangladesh.

Bangladesh is threatened by the effects of global warming since it is a low-lying country already prone to flooding.

Follow it through: climate change

Industry and transportation produce carbon dioxide and other greenhouse gases

Greenhouse gases trap more of the sun's heat inside Earth's atmosphere

A coal-fired power plant. The burning of fossil fuels is thought to be a major contributor toward global warming.

Who is to blame? A few decades ago, power plants and other industrial activities emitted the highest levels of carbon dioxide and other gases into the atmosphere. Today, experts generally agree that the increase in passenger and goods transportation by road and air worldwide contributes significantly, although not exclusively, toward global warming.

What is being done? In 1992, in New York, some countries agreed not to increase gas emissions into the atmosphere. In 1999, they signed the Kyoto Protocol and agreed to reduce emissions. However, in 2001, the U.S. government withdrew from the Kyoto agreement, even though it contributes toward around 25 percent of global carbon dioxide emissions.

Too hot to handle? Experts estimate that even if emissions stopped now, it would take the atmosphere several decades to return to carbon levels similar to those before the Industrial Revolution.

Global warming occurs

Sea levels rise
Weather becomes more extreme
Regional vegetation changes

TRANSPORTATION

Travel in today's world has become very easy. For industries, good transportation is extremely important, not just to import raw materials from other countries, but also to export finished products around the world. It is no coincidence that more economically developed countries have the best road and rail networks in the world. They have been building roads, freeways, and new railroads since they began to industrialize.

A congested highway and plane about to land at a nearby airport. A big country such as the U.S. is particularly dependent on the use of cars and planes to cover the vast distances.

Freight transportation Every year, more than 13 billion tons of freight are transported within European countries alone. In recent years, the distances that trucks travel to carry goods have increased, with about half of the freight being transported across distances of 120 miles (200 km) and more. For big countries like Australia and the U.S., a good road network is especially important. If all of the roads in the U.S. were put into one long line, it would be more than 3.7 million miles (6 million km) long.

Because roads are so important to us, we are used to seeing them in our daily surroundings. But roads have more than a visual impact on the landscape.

Follow it through: transportation

Industrial activity expands worldwide

Increased need for good transportation

Road impact

Road impact Roads split large natural areas into smaller ones. This can make it difficult for wildlife to survive. Once habitats become smaller, animals are forced to go further in search for food and are much more easily pushed onto roads.

Vegetation is also known to change considerably alongside roads. One reason is the pollution from vehicles. Land around roads gets badly contaminated with heavy metals such as cadmium and zinc, as well as motor oil from the vehicles, particularly in areas of heavy traffic flow.

Large areas of paved surface also mean that rainwater cannot sink into the ground. Instead, it runs off onto nearby land. This can wash away the topsoil and lead to soil erosion.

Take it further

Check your local newspaper for stories about local opposition to a proposed road or other transportation development.

◆ What are the advantages and disadvantages?
◆ What was the outcome?

Sea transportation Today, freight is largely transported in big cargo ships. As ship containers have become larger, many ports are not big enough to handle the increased quantity. In some cases, people have reclaimed land from the sea to build bigger port terminals.

Big port terminals can have a massive impact on the local environment. In Southampton, UK, a proposed port terminal threatens to destroy valuable natural land and wildlife. However, if the terminal is not built, the port may no longer be commercially competitive.

Air cargo For certain industries, such as the food industry, importing fresh produce by air is vital. But building airports causes massive disruption to the landscape and may require the removal of housing, countryside, or woodland.

Shanghai is China's leading port. The harbor is more than 8.5 miles (14 km) long.

More roads, rail tracks, and airports are built

More land is cleared and paved

Wildlife is threatened
Possible flooding and soil erosion

TOURISM

As the living standard for many people in developed countries has increased, people have spent more time on recreational activities and travel. Tourism particularly affects landscapes such as forests, mountains, lakes, and coastal regions, but it brings benefits as well as drawbacks.

Slippery slopes Some areas are well-known for their ski resorts: Colorado in the U.S., Canada, and the French, Swiss, and Italian Alps. Such resorts need hotels, transportation, nearby airports, and people. But skiing can also damage the local landscape. Forests are cleared to make room for ski runs that need to be prepared daily during the winter season. This damages the vegetation and leaves the soil exposed. Wind and rainfall can then easily wash the soil away.

Ski slopes in France (*above*) attract thousands of visitors each year but can cause damage to the mountain slopes (*left*). The pressure on slopes damages vegetation, causing soil to dry out and increasing erosion.

Treading carefully But even simple, high-volume activities such as hiking can have a visible impact on the landscape. Increasing numbers of recreational walkers have changed vegetation and caused soil erosion. In popular hiking areas, parking lots and improved road access have to be built, using up green space in a natural area.

Follow it through: tourism

> Tourist industry increases

> Tourist areas are developed further

Conservation

However, tourism can lead to landscape conservation as well. The creation of national parks, such as those in the U.S., has led to the conservation of huge areas that gives millions of people access to the natural landscape. Museums and visitor centers in these areas help people to learn about the importance of the parks. The money that the parks make from entrance fees can be used to create new parks as well as maintain the existing ones.

Eco-tourism

An increasingly popular tourist industry is eco-tourism. Here, local tourist operators ensure that the local environment is managed sustainably, natural resources are conserved, and tourism does not adversely affect the well-being and livelihoods of local people.

In Venezuela, private groups joined the government to form eco-travel agencies that offer special adventure tours to allow people to visit its natural, unspoiled national parks without causing damage. Experts on the tours explain to visitors the importance of the natural environment and wildlife.

Yosemite Park, California. All of the National parks in the U.S. have clearly marked paths. Signs are put up along those paths urging visitors not to walk across the open park area, since this can severely damage the soil and vegetation.

Tourist areas are managed sustainably ➤ Area is improved ➤ Tourism increases

Tourist areas are not managed sustainably ➤ Area is damaged ➤ Tourism declines

HI-TECH INDUSTRIES

One of the most rapid industrial developments of recent years has been the hi-tech industry, including electronics, electrical items, medical products, and technical instruments. This has led to the building of new, large technology parks in green-space areas.

Hi-tech industry in Bangalore, India. Asian countries are particularly successful at combining technical expertise with cheap manufacturing of electronic goods in close proximity.

Technology Technical expertise can be shared easily worldwide, and hi-tech industries are not very dependent on specific locations. But they do tend to be located either next to or close to universities because they work closely with research experts to develop technology in their specific field. A technology park can cover a wide area of land by combining management, research, training, and finance in different buildings in one park.

Manufacturing Depending on the size of the company and how much the technology park has been developed, some parks also include a separate area for the hands-on manufacturing of hi-tech products. Technology parks in less economically developed countries, such as Mexico and India, usually include a manufacturing base because land, labor, and production costs are cheaper.

Follow it through: hi-tech industry

Technology develops

More demand for electronics and communication products

Location, location, location
Since technology parks tend to be very large, they are usually built on green spaces in areas where there is already a good transportation network to attract commuters. They can also stimulate the development of large new residential developments and leisure facilities to enable local workers to enjoy their working and living environment in the same way as they would if they worked in a city.

But access to airports is another important location factor. The large computer firms of IBM, Oracle, and Apple in southeastern England have located close to the freeway servicing Heathrow airport.

Promoting the local area
Technology parks rarely cause controversy in terms of the amount of green land they use. This is because they can make the area attractive for investment. Technology parks also do not cause the same harmful impact on the environment as traditional heavy industry does, and they are often attractive and well-planned.

An aerial view over Silicon Valley, California. The area has been dominated by hi-tech industries since the 1960s.

Technology parks are created ⟩ More land is developed into road networks, housing, and parks ⟩ Green space is used ⟩ Fringes between urban and rural areas expand

BIG BUSINESS

Multi-national companies probably control about two-thirds of the world's economic activities. They begin as big companies in their own country, then gradually buy smaller companies abroad to become multi-national.

A Bangkok car factory. Thailand has greatly expanded its industrial activities as Western firms have invested there.

Manufacturing abroad Multi-nationals usually have their headquarters in a developed country, but move their manufacturing process to a less economically developed country to reduce their production costs. Sometimes they may also choose these countries because the governments there may not have adequate legislation to protect the environment. They may, for example, have weak laws or no laws at all that require industries to dispose of waste in a responsible manner. Companies, therefore, do not have to spend money on waste disposal. Or, there may be weak laws protecting the rights, health, and safety of the workers in the factories that companies can exploit. Because of their size and power, multi-nationals have a particular impact on the landscape.

Follow it through: multi-nationals

Multi-nationals look for cheap production costs

They move their production plants to LEDCs

Land pressure A multi-national production **plant** is usually set up in a sizeable town or city where there is a readily available workforce. A plant requires large amounts of land, and more land will most likely be developed for extra housing for the workers and improved transportation.

The presence of multi-nationals also attracts more people to the area in search of work. This also causes extra pressure on land resources. Not everyone may find work, and many people may end up in poor settlements in nearby towns.

Multi-nationals may also attract other local industries to the area to supply it with natural resources or product parts.

Moving on Sometimes more than one multi-national sets up production in the same area. Over time, the area will develop economically, and the local population will expect higher earnings.

A multi-national may then decide that production costs are too high and move production to another country. Because multi-nationals are so big and important, the area can then quickly decline. Industrial waste may be left, and workers may be unable to find new jobs.

A factory owned by a multi-national on the Mexican border. The conglomeration of U.S. multi-nationals in the area has been a major pull-factor for Mexican workers.

Case study: multi-nationals in the Rio Grande valley, Mexico

Since the 1970s and 1980s, the border between Mexico and the U.S. has been home to many U.S. multi-nationals with large numbers of Mexican workers. In Tijuana, a Mexican industrial town close to San Diego, there are thought to be 1,000 foreign production plants.

Future

There are signs that some of the Western multi-nationals in the area may move their manual production plants to other countries where production would be cheaper, such as Honduras or El Salvador. Already, more sophisticated industries are moving in. Korean and Japanese firms are now manufacturing more advanced, electronic products in the area, but the low-skilled, manual parts of production have been moved to Guatemala.

They choose larger towns with good transportation ➤ Industrial developments grow and attract more workers ➤ The area becomes more urbanized

INDUSTRIES AND THE USE OF WATER

The world has a limited supply of fresh water. Experts estimate that global water consumption is doubling about every two decades. The use of water by industries is an important part of this. While most water shortages around the world are due to large amounts of groundwater being pumped to farm the land, industries play a role as well. With increased industrialization in less economically developed countries, industrial water use is thought to be increasing rapidly.

Affecting the natural cycle In a natural landscape, water from rivers and lakes evaporates into the air. This eventually falls as rain that nourishes the roots of plants in the soil. Ever since people have settled along rivers, human waste has affected the quality of river water. Since industrialization, industrial waste has further affected natural waters.

With increased urbanization, large areas are increasingly being sealed off and covered with concrete. During heavy rainfall, large amounts of water can run off of concrete surfaces, taking along dust, chemicals, oil, and other pollutants that, in turn, end up in rivers.

Many industries, such as this chemical factory, are located near natural waterways or water sources. This is not only because industries use huge amounts of water in their production processes, but also because they can easily transport heavy goods along rivers.

Follow it through: water use

Industry increases

More land is sealed off

More water is used

Industry over agriculture

In some countries, water shortage is so acute that people have to reduce the amount of water used for farming in favor of industries and growing urban populations. Northern China, for example, now has to import food from abroad since it cannot afford to use water from parts of the Yellow River for agriculture, but needs to use it for its expanding industries.

Water industries In many countries, private water companies keep fresh water clean and safe for consumption. They also have to make water available to everyone by maintaining water pipes and water reservoirs. A lot of water is lost every year by water pipes that leak or burst.

Many water industries today charge for the amount of water consumed by volume rather than a straight fee. In the U.S., this has caused water consumption overall to decrease considerably. Industries reuse much of their waste water because it remains unfit for drinking even after it has been cleaned.

Recycling Some scientists think that the fear of future worldwide water shortages is irrational, and that the water issue is more about people having equal access to fresh water rather than the lack of it altogether. They argue that water can be **recycled** endlessly if water treatment methods are efficient enough, and water quality controls are carried out.

Low water in the Yellow River, Northern China. Because of the rapid increase in urbanization and industrial development, too much water has been extracted.

Cape Flats waste water treatment plant, Cape Town, South Africa. Sewage is one of the most common pollutants of water because it is still often discharged into rivers and seas.

Water pollution increases

Water has to be cleaned

Water has to be conserved

Countries that fail to develop ways of doing this face water shortages

People have had a considerable impact on Earth's surface over the last 150 years. Experts estimate that because of human activities such as using natural resources, clearing forests and wetlands, large-scale farming, and expanding urban areas, more than 40 percent of the vegetated surface of Earth has been disturbed. This affects the natural processes in which soil, vegetation, wildlife, and atmosphere interact. These processes are called biodiversity.

Experts estimate that 11,500 square miles (80,000 sq km) of rainforest are destroyed every year in Latin America alone. This not only destroys the diverse ecosystems of the forests, but also causes widespread soil erosion.

Global debate
Some people say that we should stop any activity that harms our environment and its biodiversity. But many scientists insist that land and the environment can recover from the impact of human activities as long as we manage natural resources in a sustainable way.

The food industry, for example, has seen a dramatic increase in the demand for organic foods. Organic produce is grown on small areas of land and, without the use of fertilizers or pesticides, it is less harmful to the soil and environment.

Replacing lost resources
Some industries, such as the forestry industry, are ideally placed to do their part to ensure the resources they use are being regenerated. A major U.S. flooring installation company, for example, has recently decided to start using renewable, local wheat straw as the raw material for its flooring instead of wood from tropical rainforests.

Some industries also recycle the resources they use. For example, some manufacturing industries on the U.S.-Mexican border have installed water treatment systems to recycle the water that they use in their production processes.

Follow it through: the environment

Environmental laws are made

Natural resources are replaced or recycled

An explosion in a factory in the Netherlands that caused major environmental pollution. Although industries in many developed countries can be fined for causing pollution by their production processes, they are not responsible for the cost of dealing with waste caused by their products once they are sold.

Environmental laws

Many countries today have laws and regulations in place for specific industries to follow in order to protect the environment and the land. If they violate these laws, governments can force industries to close down. For industries that inevitably have an impact on land, such as the mineral and coal mining industries, laws are important to ensure that the impact is kept to a minimum.

Some companies also promote environmental products without being forced by law. In Indonesia, coal with a very low level of sulphur and ash is supplied by a mining company. Using this type of coal reduces air pollution.

Business sense

Many industries have realized that promoting more sustainable ways of production can actually create substantial, long-term cost-savings for them. An aluminium smelter plant in Victoria, Australia, introduced ways of cutting down the amount of waste it would send to landfill sites. In doing so, the company managed to reduce its costs of waste disposal from more than $1 million to about $200,000 within a period of seven years.

Pollution is kept to a minimum

Industries save money

Impact on the land is reduced

ETHICAL INDUSTRIES

It is not only established industries that have tried to minimize their impact on the land and environment. The debate about sustainability has, in fact, created a new type of industry called ethical industry.

Fairtrade

Fairtrade means that retailers buy directly from local farmers, paying them a higher price than they would otherwise get if distributors were involved. Buying fairtrade products can make a considerable difference in the way products are grown.

But for a product to be given the fairtrade mark, farmers also have to ensure that it is produced in a sustainable way. On a fairtrade citrus farm in Cuba, the extra money the farmers receive is being spent on keeping the soil in good condition, ensuring that water sources are not overused, and that community homes and facilities are repaired.

Alternative industries

Experts on sustainability issues predict that in years to come, people will increasingly adopt changes in their daily lives that will promote more sustainable, alternative industries. In some countries, such as the Netherlands and Denmark, the bicycle manufacturing industry has expanded as more people have chosen to bike to work rather than drive. Such a trend can reduce the need for new road developments and minimize the impact on green spaces in and around cities.

Cyclists in Amsterdam, the Netherlands. The requirements of cyclists have been incorporated into the country's transportation policies. Roads are built with separate bike lanes and bicycle traffic lights.

Follow it through: sustainability

People are concerned about the environment

Customers can decide to buy products that promote sustainability

Ethical banking Consumers also drive the expansion of ethical banking. Many people have switched their bank accounts to ensure that their money is invested into ethical industries. This not only minimizes the impact on the environment, but also actively promotes it. An ethical bank may, for example, not invest any money in industries that extract fossil fuels, emit chemicals into the environment, or overuse natural resources.

Take it further

How do you know whether a business or industry is ethical? How can you find out? You could start by contacting an environmental charity or searching the web for "ethical consumer."

◆ Pick an industry that is important in your local area. Try to find out how ethical it is.

Sustainable logging using a cart horse to minimize the damage to the local forest in Germany. Sustainable logging can also mean that new trees are planted to compensate for the trees lost through logging.

Renewable energy industry More and more energy companies are offering their customers the option to buy electricity from renewable energy sources. The principle is that if customers choose energy from alternative sources, this will lead to more investment in alternative energy.

Many predict that in the future, there will also be an expansion of manufacturers of solar panels and wind turbines for home use. The UK government, for example, intends to create 10 percent of all energy produced from renewable energy sources. Since there is not enough renewable energy available to facilitate industries to use alternative energy on a large-scale, the idea is to promote more alternative energy use in private homes.

Case study: Divine Chocolate

Many food industries, particularly in chocolate and coffee, have been able to make themselves both profitable and ethical.

The Divine Chocolate company was set up in 1998 and it is partly owned by cocoa farmers in Ghana. They insure that the cocoa is grown in an environmentally friendly and ethical way. For more information, look at www.divinechocolate.com.

Ethical industries expand

A sustainable approach to industry is encouraged.

GLOSSARY

Carbon dioxide A naturally-occurring gas that consists of oxygen and carbon. It is produced when fossil fuels are burned.

Export To sell goods or services to another country.

Fossil fuels Coal, oil, and natural gas are fossil fuels that were formed underneath Earth many thousands of years ago.

Geothermal Describes the internal heat underneath Earth's surface.

Globalization The process of interaction among countries around the world in trade and communications.

Heavy industry The activity of large factories producing heavy materials such as steel.

Hydroelectricity Electricity produced with the use of water.

Import To buy goods and services from another country.

Land degradation The deteriorating conditions and quality of soil or the way land is used.

LEDCs Less economically developed countries. Countries that did not industrialize as early as the U.S. or Europe and are now in different stages of industrialization.

Light industry The activity of factories using light, raw materials to make goods, such as the textile industry.

Migrate To move from one area or country to another.

Monocultures Large, agricultural farms concentrating on growing only one type of crop.

MEDCs More economically developed countries. Countries that industrialized early and are now wealthier than other countries in the world.

Plant A site or factory where materials are processed.

Primary industry Using raw materials without processing them, such as farming.

Quarry A site where stone is extracted from the landscape.

Recycling The process of reusing a material or processing it into something else.

Retail industries Shops, department stores, bars, and restaurants.

Run-off	Rainwater running off of land rather than sinking into the ground. This happens particularly across sealed surfaces such as roads.
Secondary industry	Processing raw materials into a variety of products.
Service industry	Companies selling services rather than goods, such as banks and law firms.
Slag heaps	Rock waste that builds up after coal has been extracted from Earth.
Surface mining	Extracting natural minerals just below Earth's surface.
Underground mining	Extracting natural minerals far below Earth's surface.
Wetland	Landscape with numerous swamps and rich vegetation.

FURTHER INFORMATION

United Nations Environment Program
Provides information for businesses and industries on how they can take better care of Earth's environment and resources.

www.unep.org

Worldwatch
Provides information on sustainable economics and energy, as well as how landscapes are affected by human activity.

www.worldwatch.org

Center for the Study of Carbon Dioxide and Global Change
An organization dedicated to studying the effect of carbon dioxide on global climate.

www.co2science.org/center.htm

Sustainable development international
Provides information aimed at decision-makers in governments about a wide range of environmental issues.

www.sustdev.org

World energy
Provides information and data on conventional and renewable energy use for different regions across the world.

www.worldenergy.org

World bank
Works on trade issues and promotes worldwide trade development Features country-specific information on economic activities and a section on new ideas in pollution regulation.

www.worldbank.org

INDEX

WARREN COUNTY LIBRARY
HEADQUARTERS
199 Hardwick Street
Belvidere. NJ 07823